FRONT COVER
MY RETIREM?
POST OFFICE.

Selwyn Cecil Hutchinson

To, Rev. Rick Boyer
God Bless

Sebuya Lutala

SONS

of

INDENTURED

SELWYN C. LUTCHMAN

Order this book online at www.trafford.com
or email orders@trafford.com

Most Trafford titles are also available at major online book retailers.

Printed in the United States of America.

ISBN: 978-1-4669-8816-3 (sc)
ISBN: 978-1-4669-8815-6 (e)

Trafford rev. 05/08/2013

Trafford PUBLISHING® www.trafford.com

North America & international
toll-free: 1 888 232 4444 (USA & Canada)
phone: 250 383 6864 ♦ fax: 812 355 4082

DEDICATION

To all the Indentured Labourers, and their descendants who moved on. Also, my grandparents, my parents, sisters and brothers who nurtured me.

Special thanks to my wife, Tara, and my daughter-in-law, Michelle, who assisted me with the story and pictures.

God Bless!

ABOUT THE AUTHOR

Selwyn Cecil Lutchman "The Author" was born in Trinidad in 1942. He was baptized by a Canadian missionary Rev. JC Mc Donald. His parents Amos and Miriam Lutchman raise nine children. He was the third to last and straddled along to be educated and keep the faith of his parents. They were Presbyterians, and taught all the children to do good to others, and go to church.

My dad at twelve years old drove the buggy cart, to take the missionaries to villages to preach. He became tailor and then work in the oilfields. Mom was a housewife and did a lot of sewing, after toiling in the cocoa estate, with her mom and sister.

Selwyn did odd jobs and became a postman for thirty three years. He married Tara and they had two sons, Selvon and Sheldon.

They migrated to New Jersey where Tara works as a nanny and Selwyn went into security working for an armoured company. Selwyn continued his faith after serving as an elder at his church in Tacarigua Trinidad.

He serves as a deacon in NJ for three years and join the choir to go on a tour to Scotland. In 2002, Selwyn and Tara moved to Florida and continued their faith at hope Presbyterian Church. They became citizens or America 2004. Thanks to my brother's and pastors of the church.

The Exodus From India

The East Indians called the Indentured Labourers work the plantations for the British to produce Sugar, Cocoa and Coffee to be exported to England.

The Jahagis

When India was under the British rule, a very poor village called Uttar Pradesh, lived people who were very poor. They were told by the British if they leave their country and go to the islands of Trinidad and Tobago, to work the plantations of sugar cane, cocoa, and coffee, that they would be well treated. Some were very excited to go and some decided to stay at home.

The Journey

In the year 1845, the first sailboat called the "Fatel Razack" sailed with two hundred people. They were called the Jahagis, meaning poor and free. The journey was very long and some got sick and died due to unsanitary conditions. The journey took a few months and when they landed, they were put in barracks and nurse back to good health.

They were put to work in various fields; the men in the sugar cane field and the women in cocoa and coffee fields. They were paid for their labour and were called indentured labourers.

The Production

They produced sugar, coffee, and cocoa that was grounded and boiled then to ship back to England to be refined into tea, coffee and sugar. Many products were made and ship to other countries. The indentured labourers were treated with food and lodging.

The Cultures

The indentured labourers brought their cultures with them. Some were Hindus and some Muslims and some Christians. They practice their festivals throughout the year and sang folk songs and religious songs called Bhagans, and also dance to the coming of spring. The Muslims observed the fasting period of "Eid" for forty days; like Christians for Easter. The British shared in their festivals and ate and dance with them to the sounds of drums.

The Canadian missionaries came to the islands in the year of 1865 and taught the east Indians to read and write in English. Doctors and Nurses came to care for them with medicine and clothing. They were taught to read and understand the bible. Some Hindi songs were translated to English and were called Christian Bhagans.

Education: The Canadian missionaries built schools and churches like the British and educated the people to work in harmony and praise their God in different ways.

The Population

Increase and the production increase, and sugar, coffee, and cocoa, were consider the best in the world. The East Indians represent half the population of Trinidad and many schools and churches were built. The Canadian Christians were called Presbyterians and were trained to teach and preach the gospel of Christ.

The Discovery

When Christopher Columbus discovered the islands in the Caribbean in the year 1492, on his fourth voyage, he name the island "La Trinity" in the name of Spain, after that the Dutch fought the Spanish and took some of the islands. The British came and fought the Dutch and took over most of the island.

Slaves

The British then brought slaves from Africa to work the sugar plantation. In 1845, the British brought the Jahagis from India and they were called the indentured labourers. They took the place of the black slaves to work the plantations of sugar, coffee and cocoa. They were given food and lodging and paid for their labour. The blacks were to put to work on roads and bridges and build houses for the British. They work in harmony together with the cultures until slavery was abolished by Britain.

Some went to the sister island of Tobago to cultivate cocoa and coffee. My grandma and sister work in the fields and produced the best cocoa in the world. The British built coca houses ten feet tall; on one pillar with sliding roof to dry the cocoa pods. It is then taken to the mills to be grounded and boiled, then made into cocoa bars, to be ship back to England and other countries. Sugar and coffee were also exported to be refined and made into other products like tea, coffee, and chocolate sweets.

Teachers and Education

They were very important to the British, Canadians and indentured East Indians. Teachers produced many skills and talents like tailoring, shoemaking, carpenters, masons, gardener, farmers, shopkeepers, and many more. In the later years like Doctors, Lawyers, Judges, Policemen, Firemen, Bankers and Money Lenders.

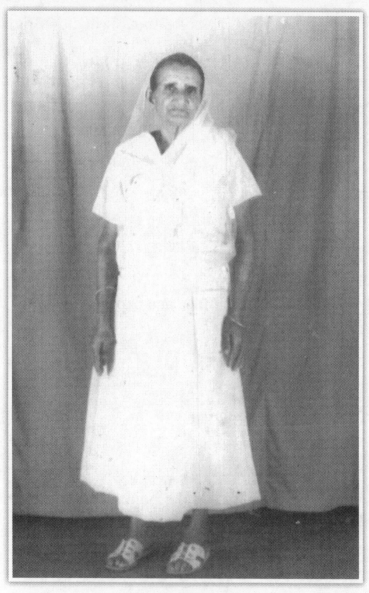

Granma Ramphal
passed in nintys 90's

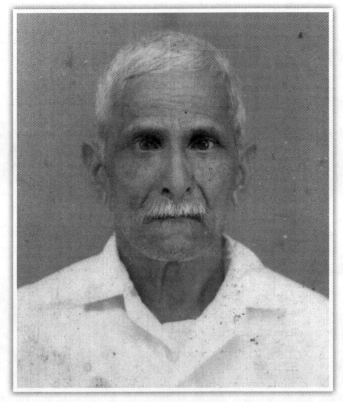

Granpa Ramphal

Generation after generation

Moved on to be successful in different fields and skills. Some reach the highest position in the country such as Prime Minister and President. Some establish high position in other countries. The indentured labourers live in harmony with other races—the Blacks, Chinese, Spanish, and Whites from England.

Independence

For Trinidad and Tobago came in 1962. The British trained the people to govern the country. A Governor General and Prime Minister were appointed and election was held to have an opposition party to bring concerns of the people.

Laws

New laws were made and police and soldiers were trained to keep the law and obey them.

Progress

The country progress with 44% Blacks, 45% East Indians and 11% of mixed with Spanish, Chinese and Whites. Trinidad is next to Venezuela and we exchange students to learn English and Spanish. Some Europeans came and settled in the country. Different cultures were recognized and different holidays were given by.

The Government

Trinidad produces oil and asphalt and has two refineries. There is a big lake with asphalt boiling like a volcano. The government digs out the asphalt and boiled it then it is put into barrels and placed on badges to be exported to other countries. Oil and gasoline is also exported with other products.

Richest Island

Trinidad and Tobago produced many different products like cement, steel, ammonia, flour, bananas, citrus fruits and vegetables. My Grandma and sister (aunt) work in the cocoa fields in Tobago. My Grandma and Aunt bought property and animals in Tobago. They work very hard in the estate and still had time to tend the cows so that they can get milk to drink and for tea. The British also enjoyed the tea and milk and other products that was planted.

The Hurricane

When hurricane Flora came in the 60's, my Grand Aunt lost all her cows in the sea. The houses were blown down and the crops were damaged. The British help them build their houses and they replanted cocoa and coffee to be exported. They pick the cocoa, crack the hard shells and cut out the pods to be put on the roof of the cocoa houses.

The Cocoa Houses

Is about ten feet tall built by the British so that the wild animals would not get them. The roof of the cocoa houses slide on rails to cover them in the night. It is dried for days then crush in the mills and boiled into cocoa bars to be ship out to England and other countries. The indentured labourers got cocoa bars to make cocoa tea and other sweet.

My Grandma Bessie (104
yrs. old), father's side and
brother-in-law, Holly

My Mother

Work the cocoa estate in the early twenties. My grandma
got sick and my mom at twelve years old had to do her
mom's task. My grandma had five children and my
mom was the eldest. They all grew up in Trinidad in the
princess town area. My grandma bought property there
and had cows in the fields. Two uncles work in the oil
field and one was a farmer. My mom's sister works in the
estate and had her family.

My Dad Amos

The Lutchman Family

My dad was a tailor in the tabaquite area and came to Tobago to see my mom and asked to marry him. They got married and had nine children; five boys and four girls. I was third to last. This is the story of descendants of the indentured labourers who made a lot of sacrifices and progress from time to time to achieve their goal. A son of the many indentured labourers, many families progress and moved on. This is the story of one family. The Lutchman family continues and grew to five generations.

My Mom

My eldest sister Bernise was a nurse at San Fernando Hospital. She helped my dad to support her brothers and sisters in school and food. Bernise work at Coura Sanitoriam Hospital and then married to Carl Howard and migrated to England. They had two sons, Jonathan and Keith. Carl Howard died in Trinidad and Bernise continue to work and moved to Vancouver, BC where she died.

My eldest brother, Thomas went to college and became a teacher. He taught at many schools and then was promoted to be principal of the Vistabella Presbyterian School. After he retired, his wife Florabelle followed her ambition and after teaching was promoted to principal at the same school. They had one daughter, Frances who has studied abroad and is back with her parents.

My mother and brothers Thomas,
Carl and Selwyn

My Granma
Sisters and brothers

Front row (L-R)   Back row (L-R)
Janet   Granma Bessie   Kenneth   Thomas
Sylvia   Bennise   Selwyn   Carl
Irene   Mike

My other brother, Mike work in the oil field as a draughtsman and then migrated to England. He furthers his studies and became an Engineer. Mike got married to Maria, an Italian woman and had three children, Michael, Mario and Monique. Mike moved to Michigan and continues working with Edison Construction Company until he retired. Mike lost one son but raise four generations.

Kenneth, my other brother also works in the oil fields as apprentice and then migrated to England to further his studies. Ken went into computers and program computers for banks in England. Ken got married to Bibi and they have three children, Susan, Darren and Andrea. Ken also works with Eastern Airlines until closed. He then went into real estate and laundry.

The Lutchman Brothers (L-R)
Carl, Selwyn, Kenneth & Mike

Irene, my other sister got married to Shaffie and raised three sons: Allan, Franklyn and Roger. Irene, a housewife learns many skills like cake icing, flower arrangement and cooking. Irene passed away at sixty years at Agnes St. Marabella, two sons in Canada.

My other sister, Sylvia got married soon after Irene and raised six children: Ian, Larry, Dave, Anthony, Robert and Donna. Robert died at nineteen years and Sylvia also learns many skills as a housewife. Her husband Raymond (Holly) Bachansingh also work in the oil fields and moved up to be supervisor then retired at home.

Janet, my younger sister was the teasing one. She was at college when our dad died and my elder brother Thomas decided to send her to England to join Bernise and study nursing. Janet got married to an intern doctor and English man and raised three children: Michael, Richard and Pauline. They both are retired and Paul became very sick. Janet lives in Kent England.

Carl, my younger brother, the baby in the family went to college and studied Business Management. He worked with banks and then got married to Sandra, a teacher. They have two daughters, Carla and Kiri. Carl and family migrated to Canada and continue to work in the bank as an Accountant. Carla is married to a Frenchman and Kiri would be following soon.

My Family
Sheldon, Selvon, Me and Tara

Granpa Sooklal
Date of Birth 1894 (Aja)
Died July 2, 1980—93 yrs

My Inlaws
Two Generations

This is the Story of my Life

I am Selwyn Cecil Lutchman, the third to last and I was struggling along going to school barefoot and behaving naughty at times. I got into a lot of fights in school; not my fault. The boys pick on me and I let them have it. Selwyn A Welch name means peacemaker. Selwyn likes sports and became very active in school. He won the Victor Lodurum Prize for the most points in sack race, three legged, cycling, flat 440 yards and house system relay. He also captains the cricket and soccer teams. My greatest ambition was artwork and essay writing. My teacher selected my essay on water. I wrote 500 words and entered the school competition. My school grant-memorial placed third in the county and I was given a prize—a very good book.

One day the Rev. Newbury, a Canadian missionary who was the pastor of the church came to my school and asked the principal to talk to some boys. He wanted to form a YMCA youth club. Twenty boys were selected of different religion and we met on Wednesday under the manse to learn different trades. He got tutors from the Salvation Army to teach us tailoring, shoemaking, bookbinding and making reading lamps from drift wood from the sea. We were taught bible study and to perform human pyramids.

We took part in sports, and did camping in the country areas for a week. Selwyn took the postman exam after one year. I was appointed a postman and work in many areas of the country. I work at the airport dispatching mails to the airlines for all countries. I was promoted to postal inspector of postmen after thirty three years of service. Slow would you say, Selwyn married Tara which was arranged and raised two sons: Selvon and Sheldon.

My elder son Selvon picking mangoes

Selvon studied hard and became an avonics technician with the national airline. He then moved on to work in many other fields after the airline lay off workers. He is now into the pharmacy business managing and training.

My Loving Daughter-in-law Michelle with mangoes from her backyard. (sweet)

Sheldon my younger son in
N.J. at School ROTC

Sheldon migrated with his mom to New Jersey. Tara was
a nanny in a Christian home and Sheldon went to school
there. Later he works with Tara's boss making wood dash
for cars. He also went into his own business of landscaping
after he sold out. He works in a pest control business with
guys from Trinidad who owns the business "Lady Bug".
After I left the post office, I join my family in NJ and did
odd jobs there like pumping gas and working as a janitor
in two churches. When I got my green card, I went into
security. I work with an armored company as a guard,

driving and picking up money from customers. We moved to Florida in 2004 when we became citizens of America. I continued to do security with Dunbar Armored and then I work at the court house CJC with a private company budd group contracted by the court. We work along the bailiff in screening people coming in to the court. I work three shifts and enjoy my job.

Tara My Wife a Babysitter
NJ & FL

Selwyn also worked in gated areas, hospitals and hotels. Being a security guard is risky.

My church in Trinidad with Lincoln & Rose
my son's God parents

21st Anniversary of the Men's Group at
Tacarigua Presbetyrian Church, Trinidad

My spiritual life started in Trinidad where I was tutored in prayer group, men group, choir and serving as an elder for eight years. In NJ, I serve as a deacon for three years and joined the choir to tour Scotland. Coming to Florida, we continued to be active in greeting, singing duets and doing lay reading from time to time.

My Church in Clearwater FL

We were a team doing visitation and singing in Trinidad, New Jersey and Florida. In Florida, we lived in a senior park called Ranchero Village. They got a gym where I work out. There are pools and games and I ride my bike sometimes to exercise. As an elder in Florida, I was the first coloured person to serve in an all white church.

Hope Presbyterian Church reminded of my home church Tacarigua Presbyterian in many ways; very friendly and cooperating.

Pastor Laura and Pastor Bob at Hope
Presbyterian Church elw. FL

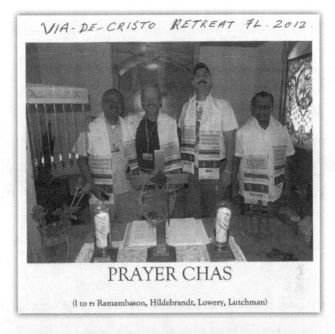

VIA-DE-CRISTO RETREAT FL. 2012

PRAYER CHAS

(l to r: Ramambason, Hildebrandt, Lowery, Lutchman)

I was introduced to a retreat in Brandon called "Via De Christo" means "The Way of Christ". It stated in Spain by the Catholics and came to America and handed to the Lutheran Church. All churches were involved and there were two weekends for the year. One weekend was for men and one for women. A rector and rectora were appointed for the weekend and a team of workers meet to arrange duties and get candidates for the weekend. We sleep in cabins with toilets and baths and dine in a large dining room. Candidates came from different churches and learn bible study and the environment in serving the community far and wide.

Spiritual directors were there to guide us and train us to serve the community. Most workers were called "Cha's". There is a musical cha's, prayer cha's, working cha's, in mail room, computer room, palanka (gifts_ and table leaders. Royo orspeakers do talks in the rollo room. Cha's serve them. I always enjoy teaching togetherness and serenity of the camp site.

Back at the hope church, Tara volunteered to baby sit the kids during service. She likes kids and has been babysitting for twenty years in NJ and Florida.

My 70th birthday was celebrated at the Holiday Inn Express in Largo. Three brothers came with their wives and stayed in the hotel. My elder son came from Trinidad with his lovely wife, Michelle. Cousins from Canada came and my wife's niece Lisa and family were there. My friend Kenneth and daughter were invited to share my joy. The brothers did a barber shop group and sang folk songs from Trinidad. There were lots of food and speeches were made.

Historic Trinidad and Tobago

Made history in sports, music, dance, carnival, artwork, and beauty. Two times Miss Universe and one time Miss World. Cricket was the most popular sport and football (soccer) which was represented worldwide.

Carnival in Trinidad
Son and Wife
Selvon & Michelle
Anita & Johnathan
Russel & others

Festivals

Carnival was advertised all over the world and the steel pan music was introduced by the Blacks. They also did a lot of artwork in metal and wood. East Indian culture continues with music and dance. The Tassa drums were very popular at weddings and parties. Different type of dances was introduced by senior and the young generations.

DIWALI in TRINIDAD

Diwali is one of the biggest festival of Hindus celebrated with great enthusiasm and happiness in India. The festival is celebrated for five continuous days, where the third days is celebrated as the main Diwali festival or 'Festival of lights'. Different colorful varieties of fireworks are always associated with this festival. On this auspicious day, people light up deyas and candles all around their house. They perform Laxmi Puja in the evening and seek divine blessings from the Goddess of Wealth. The festival of Diwali is never complete without exchange of gifts. People present diwali gifts to all near and dear ones.

THE CLAY POTS (DEYAS) ARE FILLED WITH OIL & LIT AT 6.00 PM

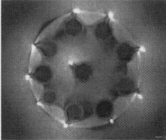

SOME INDIAN SWEETS SERVED ON DIWALI

Ramleela 2008

Ramleela, a folk theatre version of The
Ramayana, the ancient Sanskrit epic
recounting the journey of the Hindu God
Ram, is reenacted each year in various
Hindu communities throughout Trinidad.
This year the village of Felicity, whose
savannah is shown in the image attached,
celebrates 93 years of hosting Ramleela.

PHAGWA

PHAGWA, a Hindu religious festival filled with colours, songs, music and dance, will be celebrated in grand style throughout Trinidad and Tobago this weekend.

The observance of Phagwa or Holi as it is known, was introduced to Trinidad by indentured East Indian labourers around 1845. By the late 19th and early 20th centuries, Chowtal groups were growing in numbers in Trinidad and Tobago.

Phagwa is celebrated with the throwing of abir and gulal (dusts), in all possible colours. The squirting of coloured water using pichkaris (plastic pumps) is common. Coloured water is prepared using Tesu flowers, which are first gathered from the trees, dried in the sun, and then ground up and mixed with water to produce a coloured liquid.

The origin of Phagwa or Holi can be traced to the Hindu holy scriptures Vishnu Purana in which there is the story of an evil King Hiranyakashipu who wanted to destroy his own son Prahalad for worshipping God and not himself (the king).

According to the scriptures, Hiranyakashipu plotted with his sister Holika to destroy the child Prahalad by fire, for being disobedient to him. Instead, Holika perished in the inferno while Prahalad survived, thus establishing victory for good deeds over evil.

TRINIDAD CARNIVAL

The government of Trinidad & Tobago is known for its rich culture, one feature of which is the annual carnival. In the ranking of best carnivals of the world this holiday island occupies the second place after the legendary Brazilian carnival.

Trinidad & Tobago carnival is the biggest carnival of its type in the world. Similar carnivals are held in many Caribbean islands including Grenada, St Lucia, St Vincent and the Grenadines, Antigua and Barbuda, Barbados and Dominica, but Trinidad and Tobago carnival is more elaborate by far. In fact most of the smaller islands are known to be followers of Trinidad & Tobago, borrowing ideas from TnT. The twin island republic has a strong influence on English speaking islands in the Caribbean region and many carnivals are patterned after Trinidad carnival.

Hats off to all the soca artists because they're the ones who really make Trinidad & Tobago carnival what it is. Soca music is the very essence of carnival celebrations. While calypso, chutney soca, rapso and ragga soca all have their place, soca music is a leader by far.

Having mentioned soca, it would be remiss of me to leave out **chutney music**. Chutney and soca chutney has a strong connection to India and is very popular amongst Trinidad & Tobago's Indian community. The genre makes use of Indian instruments, the dholak, harmonium and dhantal, and is uptempo and very rhythmic in nature.

Current Chutney soca artists include Rikki Jai, Ravi B, Devanand Gattoo, Rakesh Yankaran, and Heeralal Rampartap.

Leading Soca artists like Machel Montano, Destra Garcia and Bunji Garlin are known to have collaborated with Chutney artists for Trinidad carnival.

The Indentured Labourers

They celebrate the coming of spring by assembling in parks to spray coloured water and powder on people. They enjoy the celebration ("Pagwa"). Ramleela was celebrated in parks to tell the story of the saints and the evil God. Diwali is the festival of lights. The Hindu people fasted for weeks and clean their homes so that the goddess Laxmi will bring light into their houses. There is a lot of food cooking and sharing to others. Christmas time the Spanish people celebrated their culture by going to homes and parks to sing and dance to the Parang music. They cook a lot of food and drink their rum to entertain the family and friends. There was also the Labour Day celebration by all races in the country.

My visit to Tobago (Roots)

This is a landmark where my parents were born
many years ago in Trinidad Tabaquite

After many years I came home from Florida and visited
my son Selvon and Michelle.

I decided to visit Tobago to seek my roots and write a
story about the indentured labourers who came from
India to settle on the islands. I discover that the old cocoa
estate has been abandon a long time ago when Trinidad
and Tobago got independent in 1962. The British had left
and no one continue the process. Some people whom I
met remember my grandma and aunt who work in the
cocoa fields.

Cocoa estate in Tobago
1930

Christina Gobin
Working the cocoa estate in Tobago

A new cocoa estate started by Mr. Dwayn Dove who bought land on the hills and replanted cocoa. I met Dwayn and he told me two sisters Christina and Nan Gobin is working for him. They were descendants of the indentured labourers.

Agayle Waterfall, Tobago

They remember my grandma and her sister who still has property there. I tour the estate and the Agale waterfall with a tour guide and bath at the falls. The tour guide sold me some cocoa ball to be made into cocoa tea—hot chocolate.

I also met Ruby McMillan who said her mother baby Seera work with my grandma.

Trinidad and Tobago continues to progress in many ways and the Jahagis who came from India to work with plantations survived and multiply in generation after generation.

The Indentured Labourer

Selwyn Lutchman

BACK COVER

WORKING AT MARRIOTT'S
HOTEL.